Kinderbunker Ltd and Soho Theatre
in association with Fat Bloke Productions
present

Julie Burchill is Away

by Tim Fountain

First performed at the Soho Theatre on 10 June 2002

Developed in association with Remy Blumenfeld and Gavin Hay

Perf
Regi

LIV

JULIE BURCHILL IS AWAY by Tim Fountain

Julie Burchill	Jackie Clune
Director	Jonathan Lloyd
Designer	Julian McGowan
Lighting Designer	Sid Higgins
Sound Designer	Rich Walsh
Production Manager	Nick Ferguson
Stage Manager	Andrea Gray
Chief Technician	Nick Blount
Production Electricians	Sebastian Barraclough
	Adrian Peterkin
Scenery built and painted by	Robert Knight Ltd

The producers would like to thank:

Pennie Smith, Anna Graf, Katharine Viner,
Toby Young, Peter York, M.T Rainey,
Ivan Massow, David Johnson,
Laura Lockington, Julie and Dan

Presented in association with

General Management Fat Bloke Productions

Press Representation Bridget Thornborrow

Advertising Haymarket Advertising

Graphic Design Jane Harper

Publicity Photography Sheila Burnett

MONOLOGUE

The Company

Cast

Jackie Clune
Julie Burchill

Jackie has appeared in the West End and nationally in her one-woman comedy cabaret shows – *Chicks with Flicks* (Edinburgh Assembly and Kings Head, London), *It's Jackie!* (Edinburgh Assembly, Drill Hall London), *Follow the Star!* (Drill Hall Christmas season) *An Audience With Jackie Clune* (Edinburgh Pleasance and Soho Theatre London) and most recently in her hit show *Bitchin'* (Edinburgh Assembly and Arts Theatre, London). Her acting credits include many years as founder member of *Red Rag Women's Theatre Company*, Sally in Bryony Lavery's play *A Wedding Story* (Birmingham Rep and Soho Theatre, London) and Carole in Dan Rebellato's one-woman play *Showstopper* (Edinburgh Assembly and Arts Theatre, London).

She toured the UK as host of *Sing-a-long-a Sound of Music* and was support act to *Puppetry of the Penis* in the West End (Whitehall Theatre) on UK tour and globally (including Melbourne and Montreal comedy festivals).

TV and radio credits include *Jackie Clune's Breakfast Show* (GLR/BBC London), T*he Lavender Lounge* (GLR/BBC London), *Front Row* (BBC Radio 4), *Broadcasting House* (BBC Radio 4) *Woman's Hour* (BBC Radio 4) *EastEnders* (Sue),*The Bill* (FME Sue Marten), *Waking the Dead* and *The John Diamond Story.* She was team captain for C4's explicit and controversial panel game *The Staying in Show.* Other TV appearances include *Richard and Judy, The Paul Ross Show, Gaytime TV, Edinburgh Comedy, Comedy Nation* and *The Jack Docherty Show.*

She is noted for her uncanny impression of Karen Carpenter's singing voice, and recorded two dance versions of Carpenter's classics *Calling Occupants* and *Close to You*, which quickly became club anthems. She is the singing voice at the front end of the hit series *Smack the Pony*, to which she has also contributed sketch material. Jackie has co-hosted and taken part in five *Stonewall Equality Shows* at the Royal Albert Hall. She lives in East London with her two scotties Lulu and Shirley.

Company

Tim Fountain
Writer

Theatre: *Harold's Day* (BAC) *Tchaikovsky in the Park* (Bridewell) *The Last Bus from Bradford* (Drill Hall/Chelsea Theatre) *Resident Alien*, starring Bette Bourne, (Bush London, New York Theatre Workshop, O.T.B Seattle, Assembly Rooms Edinburgh, Drill Hall London, Everest Theatre Sydney, The Festival Theatre Adelaide, Australia (also producer) and UK tour (also broadcast on BBC R3). Directing: *Puppetry of the Penis*, (Whitehall and two UK tours, currently Off-Broadway) *Grandmotherfucker* (Assembly Rooms, Edinburgh) *Antigone* (Birmingham Rep) *Once in a Blue Moon*, (Coventry Belgrade) *Last Bus From Bradford* (Chelsea Theatre). Television: *Bob and Margaret* (C4/Comedy Central USA - Principal Writer series 2) and *The Significant Death of Quentin Crisp* (Presenter) a documentary for C4. His biography of Quentin Crisp, was published in May 2002 by Absolute Press. Tim was Literary Manager of the Bush Theatre, London, from 1997-2001.

Jonathan Lloyd
Director

Currently Associate Director at Soho Theatre Company where he has directed *Hunting for Dragons, Hey Hey Good Looking, Jump Mr Malinoff, Jump, The Backroom, Belle Fontaine, Skeleton* and *School Play* and run writers' workshops and the Under-11s Playwriting Scheme. Other productions include *The Backroom* (Bush); *Perpetua* (Birmingham Rep); *Summer Begins* (RNT Studio/Donmar); Channel Four Sitcom Festival (Riverside Studios); *Serving It Up* (Bush); *Blood Knot* (Gate) and *Function of the Orgasm* (Finborough). As a writer for children's television; *Dog and Duck* (ITV) and *You Do Too* (Nick Junior).

Julian McGowan
Designer

Julian McGowan trained at the Central School of Art and Design. His recent design work includes: *Resident Alien* (Edinburgh festival and tour), *Feelgood* (Garrick Theatre), *I Just Stopped by to See the Man* (Royal Court); *Mr Kolpert* and *Toast* (Royal Court Upstairs); *Single Spies*, *Enjoy* and *Blast from the Past* (West Yorkshire Playhouse); *Four Nights at Knaresborough* (New Vic at Tricycle Theatre); *Some Explicit Polaroids* (Out of Joint); *Waiting for Godot* (Royal Exchange Theatre, Manchester); *Our Lady of Sligo* (Out of Joint/Royal National Theatre/New York), *Our Country's Good* (Out of Joint/Young Vic); *The Censor* (Finborough Theatre/Duke of York's/Ambassadors); *Blue Heart* (Out of Joint/Edinburgh Festival/Royal Court/national and international tour); *Shopping and Fucking* (Out of Joint/ Ambassadors/West End and international tour); *The Steward of Christendom* (Brooklyn Academy of Music, New York); *Simply Disconnected* (Minerva, Chichester); *Translations* (Abbey Theatre, Dublin); *Hamlet* (Greenwich Theatre and tour); *An Experiment with an Air Pump* (Royal Exchange Manchester/ Hampstead Theatre) and *Positive Hour* (Hampstead Theatre/Out of Joint).

His other design work for the theatre includes: *Don Juan*, *The Lodger* and *Women Laughing* (Royal Exchange Theatre, Manchester); *The Possibilities*, *The LA Plays* (Almeida), *Making History* (Royal National Theatre); *Heart Throb* (Bush); *Prin* (Lyric Hammersmith/West End); *Leonce and Lena* (Sheffield Crucible); *The Rivals*, *Man and Superman*, *Playboy of the Western World*, *Hedda Gabler* (Citizens' Glasgow); *Imagine Drowning* and *Punchbag* (Hampstead Theatre); *Tess of the D'Ubervilles* (West Yorkshire Playhouse); *The Changeling* and *The Wives' Excuse* (Royal Shakespeare Company); *A Doll's House* (Theatr Clwyd); *Torquato Tasso* (Edinburgh Festival); *American Bagpipes* and *The Treatment* (Royal Court), *Sliding with Suzanne*, *Three Sisters*, *The Break of Day* and *The Steward of Christendom* (Royal Court/ Out of Joint); *Old Times* (Theatr Clwyd/West End); *Cleopatra*, *Total Eclipse* and *A Tale of Two Cities* (Greenwich Theatre).

His opera designs include: *Alessandro Stradella* (Wexford Festival), *Cosi Fan Tutte* (New Israeli Opera); *Eugene Onegin* (Scottish Opera) and *Siren Song* (Almeida Opera Festival).

Sid Higgins
Lighting Designer

Sid was a member of the National Youth Theatre prior to joining the company professionally as resident stage manager at the Shaw Theatre. After leaving the company, he developed his stage management career both on tour and in the West End, working on a wide range of productions in drama, musical theatre, opera and dance.

Technical Management work includes *A Clockwork Orange* (Royalty Theatre); *The Music of Andrew Lloyd Webber* (Prince Edward Theatre and London Palladium); *The Phantom of the Opera* (Her Majestys Theatre) and *Aspects of Love* (Prince of Wales Theatre) and several seasons with the National Youth Theatre.

General Management work includes *The Hunting of the Snark* (Prince Edward Theatre); *The Complete Works of William Shakespeare* (Criterion Theatre and two national tours); *The Bible: The Complete Word of God* (Gielgud Theatre); *Think No Evil Of Us My Life With Kenneth Williams* (National Tour); *Cyrano de Bergerac* (Lyric Theatre); *Issey Ogata – City Life* (Lyric Theatre); *Trainspotting* (Tour); *Shopping and Fucking* (Gielgud and Queens Theatres, national tour and New York Theatre Workshop); *The Snowman* (Peacock Theatre) and *Something Wonderful* (national tour) which he also designed. He toured the United States with Vuka Uzibuze and Celtic Rhythm and was the lighting designer for *Puppetry of the Penis* (Whitehall Theatre and national tour), and *Resident Alien*. Sid is now General Manager for the National Youth Theatre of Great Britain.

Rich Walsh
Sound Designer

Previous sound designs include: *Free, Sing Yer Heart Out For the Lads, The Walls* (Royal National Theatre); *Exposure, Under the Blue Sky, On Raftery's Hill* (co-production with Druid Theatre Company), *Sacred Heart, Trust, Choice* (Royal Court); *50 Revolutions* (Whitehall); *The Boy Who Left Home* (Lyric Studio & National Tour), *Yllana's 666* (Riverside Studios & The Pleasance Edinburgh); *Strike Gently Away From Body* & *Blavatsky* (Young Vic Studio); *Body And Soul* & *Soap Opera* (for the Caird Company), *The Baltimore Waltz* (Upstairs At The Gatehouse); *The Nation's Favourite The True Adventures Of Radio One* (Jermyn Street Theatre & National Tour); *Small Craft Warnings* (The Pleasance London); *The Taming Of The Shrew* & *Macbeth* (Japanese Tour); *Dirk, Red Noses, A Flea In Her Ear* (Oxford Playhouse); *The Wizard Of Oz, The Winter's Tale* (The Old Fire Station Oxford).

The producers would like to thank

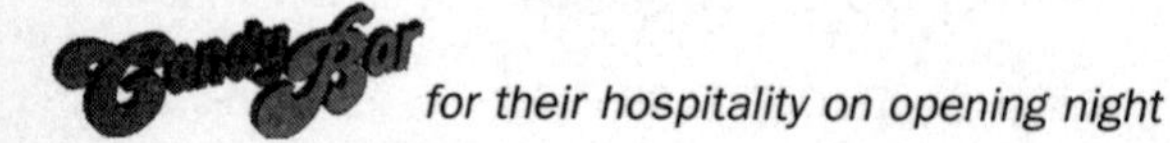

for their hospitality on opening night

Fat Bloke Productions

Associate Producer and General Manager

Productions include

666 (Edinburgh, London and International Tour)
Resident Alien (London and Tour),
Perrier Award winning Priorité à Gauche,
Noble & Silver and Scott Capurro,
The Dybbuk (JMKT Award Winner),
and the Sony Award winning
Collins Maconie and Quantick

Future productions include

Deep Throat: Live On Stage
and a season of 16 productions for Edinburgh 2002

Producers	Andrew Collier & Piers Torday
General Manager	Michelle Flower
Associate Producer	Neale Simpson

187 Drury Lane,
London WC2B 5QD

phone 020 7405 6161 *fax* 020 7405 6262 *email* f@tbloke.com

soho theatre + writers' centre

Situated in the very heart of London's West End, Soho Theatre and Writers' Centre is home to the pioneering Soho Theatre Company. Opening in 2000, the venue was a Lottery success story and quickly established itself as one of London's key producing theatres.

'a glittering new theatre in Dean Street' The Times

Soho is passionate in its commitment to new writing, producing a year-round programme of bold, original and accessible new plays - many of them from first-time playwrights.

'a foundry for new talent . . . one of the country's leading producers of new writing' Evening Standard

Soho aims to be the first port of call for the emerging writer and is the only theatre to combine the process of production with the process of development. The unique Writers' Centre invites writers at any stage of their career to submit scripts and receives, reads and reports on over 2,000 per year. In addition to the national Verity Bargate Award – a competition aimed at new writers – it runs an extensive series of programmes from the innovative Under 11's Scheme, Young Writers Group (14-25s) and Westminster Prize (encouraging local writers) to a comprehensive Workshop Programme and Writers' Attachment Scheme working to develop writers not just in the theatre but also for radio, TV and film.

'a creative hotbed... not only the making of theatre but the cradle for new screenplay and television scripts' The Times

Contemporary, comfortable, air-conditioned and accessible, the Soho Theatre is busy from early morning to late at night. Alongside the production of new plays, it's also an intimate venue to see leading comedians from the UK and US in an eclectic programme mixing emerging new talent with established names. Soho Theatre is home to Café Lazeez, serving delicious Indian fusion dishes downstairs or, upstairs, a lively, late bar with a 1am licence.

'London's coolest theatre by a mile' Midweek

Soho Theatre Company is developing its work outside of the building, producing in Edinburgh and on tour in the UK whilst expanding the scope of its work with writers. It hosts the annual Soho Writers' Festival – now in its third year which brings together innovative practitioners from the creative industries with writers working in theatre, film, TV, radio, literature and poetry. Our programme aims to challenge, entertain and inspire writers and audiences from all backgrounds.

'scorching debut brings Festival to life' Daily Telegraph

. . . on Shan Khan's ***Office*** which opened the 2001 Edinburgh International Festival

Soho Theatre and Writers' Centre
21 Dean Street, London W1D 3NE

Admin: 020 7287 5060 *Fax:* 020 7287 5061 *Box Office:* 020 7478 0100
www.sohotheatre.com *email:* box@sohotheatre.com

Soho Theatre Company

Artistic Director: Abigail Morris
Assistant to Artistic Director:
Sarah Addison

Administrative Producer:
Mark Godfrey
Assistant to Administrative Producer:
Tim Whitehead

Literary Manager: Ruth Little
Literary Officer: Jo Ingham
Associate Director: Jonathan Lloyd
Associate Director: Tessa Walker

Development Director: Carole Winter
Development Manager: Kate Mitchell
Development Officer: Gayle Rogers

Marketing Director: Isabelle Sporidis
Marketing Officer: Ruth Waters
Press Officer:
Angela Dias (020 7478 0142)

General Manager:
Catherine Thornborrow
Front of House and Building Manager:
Anne Mosley
Financial Controller: Kevin Dunn
Finance Officer: Hakim Oreagba

Box Office Manager: Kate Truefitt
Box Office Assistant: Steve Lock
Box Office casual staff:
Steven Egan, Leah Read,
Michael Wagg and Barry Wilson
Duty Managers: Beccy Buck,
Mike Owen and Kate Ryan
Front of House staff:
Morag Brownlie, Helene Le Bohec,
Sharon Degan, Meg Fisher,
Esme Folley, Claire Fowler,
Sam Laydon, Robert Mayes, Sally
Ann Moniter, Andrew O'Brian,
Rebecca Storey, Claire Townend,
Kellie Willson, Annabel Wood
and Jamie Zubairi

Production Manager: Nick Ferguson
Chief Technician: Nick Blount
Deputy Chief Technician:
Sebastian Barraclough
Technician: Adrian Peterkin

Board of Directors and Members of the Company
David Aukin —chair
Cllr Robert Davis – vice chair
Nick Allott
Lisa Bryer
Tony Elliott
Barbara Follett MP
Norma Heyman
Bruce Hyman
Lynne Kirwin
Michael Naughton
David Pelham
Michael Pennington
Sue Robertson
Philippe Sands
Eric H Senat
Meera Syal
Marc Vlessing
Zoë Wanamaker
Richard Wilson OBE
Roger Wingate

Honorary Patrons
Bob Hoskins *president*
Peter Brook CBE
Simon Callow
Sir Richard Eyre

Development Committee
Bruce Hyman – co-chair
Catherine Fehler – co-chair
Philippe Sands – vice chair
Nick Allott
David Aukin
Don Black OBE
David Day
Amanda Eliasch
Emma Freud
Madeleine Hamel
Marie Helvin
Norma Heyman
Cathy Ingram
Roger Jospé
Jonathan Lane
Lise Mayer
Michael Naughton
Barbara Stone
Richard Wilson OBE
Jeremy Zimmermann

soho theatre + writers' centre

Bars and Restaurant

Café Lazeez brasserie serves Indian-fusion dishes until 12 pm. Late bar open until 1 am. The Gordon's Terrace serves Gordon's® and Tonic and a range of soft drinks and wine.

Email information list

For free regular programme updates and offers, join our free email information list by emailing box@sohotheatre.com

Hiring the theatre

Soho Theatre has a range of rooms and spaces for hire. Please contact the theatre managers on 020 7287 5060 or email hires@sohotheatre.com for further details.

Soho Theatre is supported by

gettyimages

The Soho Theatre Development Campaign

Soho Theatre Company receives core funding from Westminster City Council and London Arts. However, in order to provide as diverse a programme as possible and expand our audience development and outreach work, we rely upon additional support. Many projects are only made possible by donations from trusts, foundations and individuals and corporate involvement.

gettyimages

Gordon's®

Bloomberg

TBWA\GGT DIRECT

A&B
Arts & Business
NEW PARTNERS

All our major sponsors share a common commitment to developing new areas of activity with the arts and with the assistance of Arts and Business New Partners, encouraging a creative partnership with the sponsors and their employees. This translates into special ticket offers, creative writing workshops, innovative PR campaigns and hospitality events.

Our **Studio Seats** campaign is to raise money and support for the vital and unique work that goes on behind the scenes at Soho Theatre. Alongside reading and assessing over 2000 scripts a year, we also work intensively with writers through workshops, showcases, writers' discussion nights and rehearsed readings. For only £300 you can take a seat in the Education and Development Studio to support this crucial work.

If you would like to help, or have any questions
please contact the Development Department
on 020 7287 5060
or at development@sohotheatre.com
or visit our website www.sohotheatre.com/development

We are immensely grateful to all of our sponsors and donors for their support and commitment.

Research & Development

Calouste Gulbenkian Foundation • The Samuel Goldwyn Foundation • The Harold Hyam Wingate Foundation • Spring Quiz Team • J J Gallagher Ltd

Education

Anon • Delfont Foundation • Follett Trust • Hyde Park Place Estate • Charity • International Asset Management • Madeleine Hamel • Mathilda and Terence Kennedy Charitable Trust • The Royal Victoria Hall Foundation • The St James's Trust • Shaftesbury PLC • The Kobler Trust • The Pitt Street Foundation

Access
Bridge House Estates Trust

Individuals

Gold Patrons • Anon • Katie Bradford • Julie & Robert Breckman • David Day • Raphael Djanogly • Jack and Linda Keenan

Silver Patrons • Anon • Rob Brooks

Bronze Patrons • Samuel French Ltd • Solid Management • Paul & Pat Zatz

Studio Seats

Anon • Jo Apted • Peter Backhouse • Leslie Bolsom • Mrs Alan Campbell-Johnson • David Day • Raphael Djanogly • Imtiaz and Susan Dossa • Anthony Gardner • Catherine Graham-Harrison and Nicholas Warren • Sally A Graudons • Hope Hardcastle • Bruce Hyman • Roger Jospé • Jeremy Levison • John and Jean McCaig • Annie Parker • Eric and Michèle Senat • Simonetta Valentini • Marc Vlessing

SOHO THEATRE + WRITERS' CENTRE

In 1996, Soho Theatre Company was awarded an £8 million Lottery grant from the Arts Council of England to help create the Soho Theatre + Writers' Centre. An additional £2.6 million in matching funds was raised and over 500 donors supported the capital appeal. The full list of supporters is displayed on our website at www.sohotheatre.com/thanks.htm

BUILDING SUPPORTERS

Supported by the Arts Council of England
with National Lottery funds
The Lorenz Auditorium
supported by Carol and Alan Lorenz

Principal sponsor: Gettyimages

gettyimages

Rooms: Gordon's Terrace supported by Gordon's Gin • The Education and Development Studio supported by the Foundation for Sport and the Arts • Equity Trust Fund Green Room • The Vicky Arenson Writers' Seminar Room • Writers' Room supported by The Samuel Goldwyn Foundation • Unity Theatre Writers' Room • Writers' Room supported by Nick Hornby and Annette Lynton Mason • The Marchpole Dressing Room • Wardrobe supported by Angels the Costumiers • The Peter Sontar Production Office • The White Light Control Room • The Strand Dimmer Room • The Dennis Selinger Meeting Room

Building: The Esmée Fairbairn Charitable Trust • The Rose Foundation • The Meckler Foundation • Roberta Sacks

Soho First: BAFTA • Cowboy Films Ltd • Simons Muirhead & Burton

Gold Patrons: Eric Abraham • Jill and Michael Barrington • Roger Bramble • Anthony and Elizabeth Bunker • John Caird • David and Pat Chipping • John Cohen at Clintons • Nadia and Mark Crandall • David Day • Michael and Maureen Edwards • Charles Hart • Hat Trick Productions • David Huyton at Moore Stephens • Miriam and Norman Hyams • David Jackson at Pilcher Hershman • The St James' Trust • John Kelly – European Quality • Mr and Mrs Philip Kingsley • The McKenna Charitable Trust • Nancy Meckler and David Aukin • Michael and Mimi Naughton • Robert Ogden CBE • Diana Quick • Christian Roberts • Lyn Schlesinger • Peter M Schlesinger • Carl Teper • Diana and Richard Toeman • Richard Wilson OBE • Margaret Wolfson

Registered Charity: 267234

Tim Fountain

JULIE BURCHILL IS AWAY . . .

NICK HERN BOOKS
London
www.nickhernbooks.co.uk
in association with

Fat Bloke Productions

ACT ONE

Present day. Lunchtime.

The living room of Julie Burchill's house, a large thirties building in Hove, Brighton.

On one side of the room is a classic period mantelpiece. On it are various old football trophies and family photos. In the centre a bust of Lenin. Above the bust on the chimney breast is the famous picture of Roosevelt, Churchill and Stalin – though on closer inspection it's been doctored and the Spice Girls have somehow interloped. At the back of the room are a set of French windows leading to the garden and swimming pool. The doors are guarded by a huge, kitsch pot leopard. At the other side of the doors an eighties uplighter with a Princess Diana tee-shirt hanging on it. On the other side of the room a wall with a picture and a shelf with five naked plastic dolls on it. Hung below the shelf is a plastic parrot which says 'Isn't Julie clever' on request. Centre stage is a large leopard skin sofa and coffee table. Newspapers and magazines are scattered around the floor. Facing the sofa is a TV which is on. The whole room is sparse and has the air of a house recently moved into, rather than fully inhabited. Sunlight streams in through the French windows which are slightly ajar. Outside we can hear the cry of seagulls. Julie is laid on the sofa in her dressing gown reading The Sun.

JULIE (*calling off*). Here Dan, a man's been killed in Australia after being stung by a jellyfish the size of a peanut. (*To us.*) Isn't that terrible? He was on his honeymoon as well. Really sad. It's amazing what you read in the papers innit? There was a piece in *The Mirror* the other day about a couple who take a meat pie on holiday with 'em. They been doin it twenty years, they've given it a name and everything. (*Calling off.*) You all right up there? How you getting on? (*To us.*) He's trying to mend my computer, It seized up last night after the letter 'I' key got jammed. It was just after I'd been banned from the *Guardian* chatroom for using offensive language. Divine retribution Dan said. I been banned three times now under different names. Maybe I should go on as myself next time and then they'd have to ban their own columnist and it could become a test case.

Picks up Daily Mail.

Oh look another riveting article about the rise of the Domestic Goddess! Someone should do a riveting article about what it's like to be married to one. Imagine it, you come home from a hard day at the office and say, 'What did you do today dear?' 'Oh I baked a cake and pruned a rosebush.' It's no wonder so many men end up going to prostitutes, at least they have some outside interests, even if it is just their crack habits. I reckon that's why so many Johns just pay to hear the broad's story, it's 'cos their own wives' conversation bores 'em to tears. What was it Jerry Hall said when her Mother told her a woman should be 'a lady in the drawing room, a cordon bleu chef in the kitchen and a whore in the bedroom'? She said, 'I'll hire a maid and a cook, and take care of the rest myself!' I like that. Although I think if I'd been married to Mick Jagger I'd have been inclined to go for a paid prostitute as well! He looks like an origami-obsessed giant got hold of him and practised for hours. Food the new sex, gimme a break, the only new sex is sex with someone new.

Checks watch.

Heavens, look at the time!

She sits up.

I gotta get moving. I'm having lunch with a hack at Sun Bo Seng. He's doing a piece on 'becoming the next Julie Burchill' for *The Times* Media Section. I said to him on the phone, do you think anybody really wants to be, it's bad enough for me! The only advice I can offer is don't work too hard. It's a fact of life that the more work you do the more people give you, and before you know it you end up looking like Ian Beale. People who work hard always claim to be martyrs, but actually they're tremendous egoists, they just want everyone to believe the world will end if they let up for one minute. When anyone rings up to commission a piece from me I always say, 'What's the least possible words by the latest possible time?' They usually laugh, but when I go silent they soon know who's in charge. If you work too hard at writing I think the readers can smell your sweat and it puts 'em right off. Look at Parson's *Man and Boy*. You can tell he's really had to struggle to produce that. Mind you if you're Tony and you write English like it's your second language I don't suppose you got much choice. Still it's been a success annit? I'm pleased for him, no I am. I'm pleased that at 49, on his fifth attempt he's finally got a best-seller 'cos I had one at 29 and jealousy's not good for a person is it? Eats you up.

What's the betting the first question this hack asks me is if I write just to wind people up. They all ask me that, really proudly, like they're the first person who's ever thought of it. If I didn't mean it I'd be full of self loathing and how can you loathe yourself when the rest of the world's doing it for you? That'd be just joining in with the crowd wunnit? I've always said what I thought, even as a kid I'd tell all my Aunties what I really thought of their outfits at family weddings. People say to me, 'But doesn't it hurt Julie when people slag you off for it?' and I say, 'No I don't give a toss.'

Picks up Guardian Weekend *mag.*

It's like all the letters people write about me in here, 'Fat dyke', 'Castrating Fascist bitch', 'Crypto Commie fuck wit', they don't bother me. My friend Mark Simpson says that's 'cos I don't actually live in this world, he says I inhabit Julieland and that's a place where no-one can hear you scream. (*Laughs.*) I like that! I even made it my e-mail address. My ex-girlfriend (and before you start that doesn't make me a Lesbian, It means I once had an affair with a woman. If you go on a day-trip to Bruge it doesn't make you Belgian does it? And it doesn't make me bisexual 'cos that's a disgusting word innit? Makes me think of suburban couples getting all sweaty and swapping wives over fondue), anyway this girl I used to go out with said the reason I didn't care was

because I was a psychopath. She said whene
saw a picture of Rose West on TV she thoug
me. Isn't that rude? She's right though I am
psychopath, or a sociopath, not sure which.
I ought to care more about other people but I just don't, and I feel bad about that which is worse, but I don't FEEL it's worse, which is bad. To me other people are just shadow puppets, I can't do empathy – why should I feel for other people – they might as well just be tables or chairs. I've always been like that. When I was four I was expelled from my nursery school for prodding the other kids during their afternoon nap and making 'em listen to me read. Well it's such a waste innit, being asleep in the afternoon when you could be out drinking or taking drugs. Still I suppose they were only four. I gotta get changed and I ain't doing it in front of you lot.

She goes out. Bobs head round door.

Feel free to talk amongst yourselves, I won't be a tick.

She re-enters wearing a black dress and top.

Do I look all right? As if I care. I've been wearing black outfits like this since I was thirteen, when I realised my Dad would eventually die. To my mind, following fashion is rather like masturbating or making silent phone calls to ex-lovers after midnight; sort of cute and inevitable when you're young, but indicates a rather tragic lack of life once you're old enough to vote. Did you see Giorgio Armani announced his next collection was going to 'pay homage to the workers, to their dignity, simplicity and straightforwardness'. As God is in the details, let's hope his catwalk models are mutilated, bleeding and tumour-ridden, because that's the thanks their dignity, simplicity and straightforwardness has brought most workers. I'll never forget years ago being at some posh dinner with Katherine Hamnett, and she suddenly pipes up saying, 'I think the young working class are much better dressed than the young middle class.' I said, 'Yes, that's 'cos they can't afford your clothes.'

That's the first thing I'm gonna tell this hack, you don't have to get all middle class to become a writer. No, but a lot of people think you do. I thought you did when I was growing up. I used to walk around my estate in Brislington dressed in black, smoking purple cigarettes and spouting Oscar Wilde. That didn't go down too well in a town where most people's career horizons made the average pit pony look like Stephen Hawking. It's true! In Brislington you were only allowed your name in the paper twice in your life, once when you were born and once when you died, anything else was considered showing off. No wonder I had a shortage of friends, but I didn't mind 'cos I wasn't looking for friends. It's a bit of a taboo to say that, isn't it? You can say you don't want a boyfriend or a wife or even that you don't want your parents (I mean you can just put them in a home. I thought a home's what they were in already so surely that's just an anti-home?) but you can't say you don't want friends. But I was an only child and I knew right from the start that when it came to my brilliant career I couldn't rely on anyone but myself. I had a copy of the tube map on my bedroom wall and I learned all the stations off by heart so I'd be ready. So beautiful that map! People say art never changed anyone's life but Harry Beck who designed that map changed mine.

I think if you wanna be a writer you gotta read a lot. I hardly read at all now, I think readings a bit like ambition, looks sad after forty. But when I was a kiddie I was a mad reader (not voracious – hate that word. 'Jenny's a voracious reader, she'll even read the cornflake packet.' Silly bitch. Who wants to read a cereal packet?!) But I loved books. Stories where there were monsters and I was a girl explorer, or where there was a future and I was middle class. Sometimes I'd have four on the go at once and I'd read them in rotation. My mother thought I was going to be a serial killer. She'd walk into the kitchen and see me at the table and burst into tears, like she'd given birth to the devil child. She just couldn't understand why I was spending all night reading when I could've been sat with her and my Dad watching Bob Monkhouse. When I started writing she'd say, 'Doing nice typing?' She wouldn't call it writing, 'cos writing was weird and dangerous. She was right I suppose, but I like the feeling of having done it: like having really excellent sex with someone you're not meant to be having it with. I think good writing's a bit like walking a tightrope. If it goes well, you get from one side to the other, but if it goes really well, you fall off and you fly. God did I just say that? Better it came out now than over lunch! That's the trouble with doing interviews about being a writer, you end up sounding like a wanker.

Fetches make-up bag in.

I bet he asks me when I'm gonna become a more 'serious' writer? They all ask me that. I tell them I'm just a hack and I'm proud to be a hack, but they don't believe me. That's what that crazy old fucking dyke Camille Paglia never understood about me when we had our stupid 'fax war'. She couldn't get her head round the fact that there was someone out there who didn't actually aspire to be her. I told her, 'I might not be as loud as you but I'm ten years younger, two stone heavier, and I haven't had my nuts taken off by academia.' That shut her up. 'English Literature.' It's impossible to say it without lisping or coming over all Martin Amis. He's a perfect example of someone who blew it when he decided he was a 'serious writer'. If he'd stuck to writing about smoking, shagging and snooker he might have been the next Nick Hornby. Have you noticed there's just two schools of male writing: the pansies and the pugilists. You're either a Parisian faggot who writes between asthma attacks or you're Hemingway and you fit it in between bull fights. If most male actors wanna be Hamlet, most male writers dream of being Hemingway. Not that you'd know it from the average English male novelist: most of them couldn't make a fist even if they had the young Arthur Rimbaud bent down in front of them begging for it. No, It's 'hack' for me. Oh I feel a like poof reclaiming the word queer!

Besides if I was a 'serious writer' I wouldn't be able to go out for lunch on a column day when I hadn't written it, would I? My *Guardian* column's due in at two-thirty. I haven't got a clue what to write. Still, if I'm back for two I got half an hour. Well I can't do it now my computer's bust, can I?! (*Calling off.*) How you getting on Dan? Do you want anything to eat? Slice of cake? Don't know why I'm saying that 'cos I ain't got anything in apart from two Marks and Sparks ready meals. There's a classic example of me simply mimicking other people's good behaviour but not really thinking it through. (*Calling off.*) I'm quite looking forward to a bit of Chinese. Stir-fried beef with black bean sauce I think. Don't tell my personal trainer. He's beautiful, he's like a dark David Beckham, but he dun half bollock me about what I eat. Trouble is I love going out for lunch, it's a naughty meal innit? In the middle of the day when you should be working. I shall have to get on my step machine in the morning! I gotta a little gym in the other room. Cross-trainer and everything, it's even got a little thing for putting your drinks in, great for parties.

I get really nervous meeting people by myself. I usually take a third person along with me, it's like I need an audience or something. I always have to pay as well. Even if they're on exes I pay. Dunno why. Maybe it's so I can do my card trick. I get both my black American Express cards out and put them on top of each other, really ostentatiously.

She does it.

There's no credit limit on 'em, apparently I could buy a Harrier Jump Jet, well I could buy two. I love being crass and eighties. My favourite crass and eighties moment was when I went to the Imperial Hotel in Torquay with Dan. 'Cos I'm working class I always carry lots of cash with me in case there's something good to buy. Anyway this day we were going down to the pool and the vodka and orange I'd mixed in the room leaked in my bag and got all my money wet. So I laid it on the sunbed to dry, unfortunately I fell asleep and rolled onto it. When

I woke up I forgot, got up to go to the pool and walked across the terrace in front of everyone with three hundred quid in ten-pound notes stuck to my back! I shall have to tell him that. It really winds 'em up when I get all crass and tell 'em how much I loved the eighties. You're not supposed to say it, are you? You're supposed to say, 'It was a terrible, greedy time and we all came to our senses in Princess Tony's caring, sharing, nineties.' My arse. If anything everything's greedier now with Blair's Sunday school capitalists ruling the roost. Tony and Mandy: the stewardship of Keir Hardie's party handed over to a small town lay preacher and Hyancinth Bucket, don't get me started.

But I do feel sorry for the eighties, every other decade has had at least some good press: the 'conformist' fifties had Frankie Sin and the dry Martini; the 'messy' sixties had the mini and the Mods; the 'apocalyptic' seventies had Biba lipstick and the sound of Philadelphia; but the eighties have been reduced to just two things things, mammon and mammaries, The Big Bang and Samantha Fox. It's true, for most of the press the ideal eighties photo-op would have been Sam Fox in leg warmers on the steps of the London Stock Exchange with her knockers out. The real story has been buried beneath the clichés of carping hacks and the platitudes of playwrights pissed off with the fact that squatting in mud at festivals went out of fashion. I lived in a different eighties, as did my mates. We weren't saints or sinners, we were just kids tired of being on the right-on, street-cred ropes with their noses pressed up against Langan's window pane wondering what *crème brûlée* was. And the eighties weren't just about aspiration, there was a whole new form of feminism: Martina Navratilova, Joan Collins, Madonna, suddenly feminism wasn't just about free cervical smearings on the NHS but the right to have as much fun, money and clout as the men. Madonna dragged feminism along in her slinking stride like a cave woman who had just killed her dinner. I tell you what, her predatory pursuit of all that life, love, and Securicor had to offer was a damned sight more inspirational to young women than all those milch cows, mouldering away at Greenham Common, every hirsute inch the passive female stereotype. What was it Shirley Poliakoff said, 'I've only got one life so let me live it as a blonde.' Brilliant! I haven't spoken to most of my eighties friends for ages. Robert Elms, Toby Young, Lesley White, must be ten years since I exchanged a civil word with any of 'em. I love it when a new feud starts; it's like a cross between mild sexual excitement and the feeling you get when the plane leaves the runway. The truth is that most people are much more fun as enemies than they were as friends or lovers. Hatred brings out the artiste in yer. When we're in love we're like junkies, just one big blissed-out mess. It's true, if someone published your love letters, you'd want to crawl away and die, because, no matter how smart you are, they'd be some variation of what Jeremy Thorpe wrote to Norman Scott: 'Bunnies can and will go to France!' But when you hate someone you're totally yourself: you're hard, you're clean, you're glinting; in fact you're everything they loved you for in the first place. There are no friends – only enemies we have yet to make is my motto. You know as a child I couldn't say the word friend, I always pronounced it 'fiend'. 'What a fiend we have in Jesus' I sang in church one Sunday. The Vicar told my mother they thought I'd developed wiccan tendencies.

Starts to apply make-up.

I suppose the thing with me is that, even though I love writing, if it comes to a choice between doing another thousand words or a nice liquid lunch with my boyfriend, there is no choice. I'm reminded of what Philip Larkin said when someone asked him why all his poems were so miserable, he said, 'When I'm happy I'm too busy having a good time to write.' I know exactly how he feels 'cos I'm a hedonist, you're gonna die so you might as well live is my motto. Hedonism and religious faith are the twin pillars of my existence. Have a great time whilst you're here and an even better one when you've gone! According to all the surveys the worst thing you can be is a sober atheist. Like all those bores who were up in arms when Daniella Westbrook lost a bit of her nose after doing too much coke. I don't know what the fuss was about, she looked better with half a nose than most of them looked with a full one. Course all the phoney columnists trotted out the 'Poor tortured Daniella' line. See, for a woman to risk her 'all important' looks for her own pleasure is a mortal sin. Brigitte Bardot's a wine-drinking, sun-seeking, mess whilst that turnip-headed man-mountain Jack Nicholson's an 'attractive older man' and Ronnie Wood (who snorted so much coke he could eventually see through his nose) is part of 'rock's rich tapestry'. I think youth and beauty should be burned up.

When you're on your deathbed it's the fun you had you'll look back on, not the youth and beauty you preserved 'cos now you're gonna die anyway! Besides Daniella's got a rich boyfriend, she can always have a new bit stuck on, can't she?

Powders nose.

Between 1986 and 1996 I put enough up my snout to stun the entire Colombian armed forces. But look at it, still there.

Looks in mirror closely.

My Dad's nose. (That was the only aspect of taking coke that ever used to freak me out. I'd get to about 3am and suddenly think, 'Fuck! I'm putting cocaine up my father's nose!') I don't regret my years as a coke head one bit; a whole decade went by in a blur, like some crazy Aerosmith video. The print media's like the theatre, the people are so dull and self-obsessed that if you don't do drugs it's impossible to get through. To me a few palpitations now and then is pretty low price to pay for not becoming Melanie effing Phillips. Someone wrote to the *Guardian* and said, 'How can Julie Burchill be bored in a world where there's so much music to listen to, so many parks to walk through, art galleries to visit.' Art galleries to visit! Oh yeah right, I forgot, who needs drugs when you got the Tate Modern! People always say to me, 'But what about your looks, don't you regret losing your looks?' I say no, when I was younger I was the sweetest chick in town, I had a 38-inch chest and a waist like this (*handspan*) and what did it get me? Tony Parsons. Now I'm ageing I've got a twenty-seven-year-old boyfriend and I'm getting it five times a night. Funny thing is, though

I hate to admit it, when I first met Tony he was actually quite impressive. No he was! I remember I walked into the *NME* office and he came straight over and, without saying a word, just lifted me up in his arms and put me on top of the filing cabinet! And he was immaculately working class. His Dad was a war hero and his Mum was a Dinner Lady. I think we literally smelled each other's blood royal. We were like two toffs meeting in the jungle and changing into their dinner-jackets without consultation. We had our own section of the office, we put barbed wire round it and a sign up saying 'DEATH TO HIPPIES'. The Editor christened it 'The Kinderbunker'. And we'd a noose above our desk and get this right, the hippies said it gave them bad vibes, and they'd take it down at night when we went home! Bless 'em. Funny thing is I hated punk. Every night I'd be sent off to see The Clash or The Ramones and all the time I'd be sat thinking, 'I wish I could listen to some Ivor Novello now'. It's true, I'd file my copy and then go home and put the Isley Brothers on. And the money was so bad me and Tony had to take empty pop bottles back to the corner shop to pay for our bus fare. If it was like today, 'no deposit, no return', we'd have never got to work. Then people said to me when I went to the *Sunday Times*, 'Oh you've really sold out.' I said, 'You wanna try living on Tizer and Frosties and see how you like it!' It wasn't just the money. I wanted mainstream fame. Being a cult figure's all right in your twenties but after that it's like being asked to someone's house for cocktails when you know everyone else is staying for dinner. You can sink or swim in the mainstream, all you can do in the margins is tread water. It was unheard of in those days to go from the pop press straight to Fleet street. You were meant to serve your time in the regions and work your way up. I wasn't having any of that. Overnight I went from spending my time in toilets in King's Cross to . . . well spending my time in toilets in Dean Street, but for a different reason! A bottle of Bollinger, a gram of coke, dinner at Langan's and you still got change out of £80,000 a year; I loved it. The eighties were my kind of decade: shallow. I had the biggest, reddest flat in the West End, a baby who looked as though he'd left his wings with the coat-check girl and my name was mentioned on *Brookside*. Karen Grant came into her kitchen and announced to her Mum, 'I'm gonna be the next Julie Burchill.' My parents were made up. Must remember to tell this hack about *Brookie*, kids'll like that story.

She picks up the phone and dials.

Hi, it's Mrs Landesman. Hello. Could I have a taxi to take me to Sun Bo Seng. Thanks. Bye

She hangs up.

I hope I get Geoffrey. Somebody was telling me and Dan the other day that Geoffrey from *Rainbow* is now a taxi driver in Brighton. I don't wanna go do this interview now. Wish I'd never agreed to it. Probably be all right when I get there.

Looks out of the French windows.

You know the other day there was this really beautiful fluffy grey duck with a really intelligent face sunbathing by my swimming pool and for some reason it reminded me of Kirsty Young. I was dead excited 'cos ever since I came to Brighton I've been trying to get a wild animal to live in my garden. Course when I told my posh pro-fox-hunting friend she said, 'Ah if you'd had a fox in your garden he'd have killed Kirsty.' I said, 'Yes but I wouldn't have minded because then I'd have had a fox in my garden.' I've always been like that see, pragmatic. Always think what I've got now is the best I've ever had.

Pause.

What am I gonna tell this hack that I haven't told a thousand interviewers before? That's the trouble with having been in the game as long as I have, I've said everything. I even bore myself saying it. I did an interview a couple of weeks back and I could hear the stories echoing in my head as I told 'em.

Beat.

I know! I'm gonna tell him one of the pre-requisites of a successful career as a writer is having a used-up marriage. That'll give him a good line. 'Burchill recommends used-up marriages to fledgling hacks.' It's true though, I think it really helps. In fact there are two good things about being in a used-up marriage, one is you get to take your make-up off every night with a nice gooey moisturiser which isn't sperm, and the other is you get a heck of a lot of work done. I wrote four books during my six years with Tony but I only wrote three during my eleven years with my second husband, 'what'shis-name', which further proves just how bad in bed Parsons really was. I'll never forget the first shag we had, the first shag I ever had. It felt like a cross between someone standing on my toe and having a tooth pulled without anaesthetic. No wonder I wrote so much. I think the Protestant work ethic got invented because Martin Luther couldn't stand doing it to Mrs Luther any more. You know the national average is 2.5 times per week? When I first saw that figure I thought it must be a misprint for 25. I can only do it three times a day or not at all. There's something about the idea of having sex 2.5 or even three times a week that makes me want to scream violently, run down the street tearing my clothing and hack out my primary and secondary sex organs. It's just so blahhhhh! I've got two sex speeds, 'mad for it' and 'why bother?' When you want someone you want them all the time, when you don't want them you don't. What's the definition of a liar? Someone who says they still really love sex with the same person after doing it regularly with them for four and a half years! My favourite divorce joke ever – apart from my life – is 'I'm not gonna bother getting married again, no to save time I'm just gonna find someone who hates me and buy them a house.'

Looks out of front window.

Come on taxi. Don't wanna be late. Like to get there first and get it all set up as I want it.

Looks again out the front window. We hear seagulls.

I love hearing the seagulls, they sound like all their PMT came at once. I think the reason they sound so sad is that each seagull contains the spirit of a Londoner who always meant to move to Brighton but died before they managed it and now they're condemned to fly endlessly in search of their final nesting place. Keith Waterhouse said: 'Brighton looks like a town which is helping the police with their enquiries.' Isn't that brilliant? To me it looks like a town which has just had a multiple orgasm whereas London looks like Bill Wyman: a sad old rocker who takes you out for a posh dinner and then can't get it up. If London does swing, it's in the manner of a hanging man. When I was in my Groucho phase I used to come here at weekends to try and recover my sanity. I'd stay in the Hotel Metropole on the front in a suite on the far left where I had a fantastic view of the ruined West Pier. I'd sit up on the balcony all night drinking hard and thinking that poor rotting structure was trying to send me a message about myself: A magnificent ruin! Course by that stage the red sign said 'West Pie' rather than 'Pier', which kind of took away from the tragedy. And then when they finally turned that off they put up a plastic banner saying 'Save me'! I really did think someone was trying to send me a message. Brighton's the first place I've chosen to live. I was born in Bristol, forced to go to London to get a life, but Brighton's the first place I chose to make my home. Oh god I just used it! (*Calling off.*) Dan I just used the word 'home'! 'Come to our home for dinner', the six most chilling words in the English language. I only bought this place 'cos my accountant told me I had to, otherwise all I earned would go up my nose. Twenty thousand pound a room, he said. There's nothing scares me more than going round to some pile in NW Twee and there's an Aga chugging away and some rough-hewn coffee table with a load of books on gardening, or Nigella Lawson or Feng Shui. 'Feng Shui!' It remains the great mystery of our age that people can have rejected something as sensible as Marxism as a means to improve their lives and yet they think that moving the furniture around can make a difference. To me, there is only one point in moving furniture and that is to procure a spontaneous abortion. (And I should know 'cos I've had so many the clinic have issued me with a loyalty card.) Look see . . .

She points to the dolls on the shelf.

Five dolls. One for each of my abortions. Where's that taxi?

Goes to phone again.

Hi, it's Mrs Landesman again. Sorry to trouble you. It's just I ordered a taxi and I was just wondering if it's on its way? Sun Bo Seng, that's right. Thank you. Bye.

Puts phone down.

What I'd really like to do now is get Dan down from upstairs, get in his car and drive off down the motorway to Torquay and to hell with it all for today. Wouldn't that be bliss? Check into the Imp. Nice swim in the pool with the underwater music. Nice dinner. Dan's great to go away with, we have such a laugh, especially when we go driving. The other day I cracked him up when I asked him what his favourite coloured traffic light was. I like the orangey ones. He's only twenty-seven but he's the first adult I been out with. He don't live with me but he's got a place just round the corner. We might get married, or we might not. I know, in spite of all I've said, but the truth is I like being married. I'm not a person who's ever single. Since I was seventeen I ain't ever been single. People say, 'But you don't need to get married Julie,' but I'm traditional. When you look at wedding photos they look so lovely don't they? The beautiful bride in her beautiful dress. The less beautiful bridesmaids in their less beautiful dresses. The dog of a Matron of Honour in a dress that only a mother-in-law bent on making a fool of a girl could love! One of the first things I did when I was old enough to know one end of a biro from another was scribble all over my Mum and Dad's wedding photos. Even if it doesn' t work out I like the idea of having lots of divorces, like Diana Dors. 'What'shisname' said I should form 'The Mr Barbra Streisand Club' for my exes because whoever I married would never be as famous as me and they could all meet up once a year and exchange stories and bitch about me. I like the idea of leaving a lot of exes behind stood round my grave, it's just so cruel. I really like this one though. I can't imagine what I'd do if he left me. He's a saint. I don't mean he don't drink or nothing – he can party with the best of them – but he has saintly qualities. He's not petty and he's not egotistical like me. When I get a new boyfriend I never bother to make up a new pet name for him and I always have the same 'special song'. Saves buying records dunnit?

Beat.

I'm only joking, I do feel like I've finally found someone I can settle with. I can't tell this hack that, can I? He still thinks I'm a 'hip young gunslinger'. I am still a hip young gunslinger!

Car horn toots.

That'll be my taxi.

Looks out.

No sign of Zippy and Bungle. (*Calling off.*) Dan I'm going! Do you think it'll be done for when I get back? Great. Bye babe.

Car horn toots again.

Alright love just a minute!

Starts to straighten her coat.

Telling someone how to become me is quite a major project, have to make sure I'm properly dressed. Right, let's give him hell, if you mess with the Bull you get the horns!

She exits, the door slams. The phone rings, the ansaphone kicks in.

'Hi this is Julie. If it's Katharine, Katharine I can't answer the phone 'cos my computer's bust and I gone down the shop for a part with Dan. It should be mended by three and then I can send my column through. I would have faxed it but it's trapped in the system at the minute. Bye. Oh, if it's anyone else leave a message.'

Katharine's voice kicks in: 'Julie we go to press at two . . . Julie! Julie pick up! Julie!!'

Seagulls squawk. Lights fade.

End of Act One.

ACT TWO

The same. An hour later.

Lights up. The room as before except a lap-top Mac now sits on the table with a Post-It note attached.

We hear the sound of a car door slamming and then a key turning in the front door. Julie enters carrying a 'Threshers' bag.

JULIE. Babe I'm back! Dan?

She enters the living room and spots the computer and Post-It note on the coffee table. She goes over and reads the note.

Bless him he's mended it.

She plonks the bag down.

That's the last time I'm going to be interviewed this year.

Takes coat off.

He was such an arse! Every question I predicted he'd ask, he asked. 'Do you try and deliberately provoke?' 'What about your children?' 'How does it feels to be described by the *Daily Mail* as Britain's worst mother?'. It feels fucking fantastic, feels a damned sight better than having done a media studies degree at Bristol University! Oh yes, he couldn't wait to to tell me he'd done a course. I felt like saying, 'Oh so that makes it all right to be boring, does it?' 'Education, education, education!'

'Useless, useless, useless' more like. It makes me puke, the middle classes squeezing the life out of everything from food to football, with the dead hand of their dreary, desiccated, deracinated taste. He's moving to Brighton as well, next thing you know he'll be one of Simon effin' Fanshawe's mates, running round getting his frillies in a twist trying to turn Brighton into the European City of Culture meantime I can't even get my bins emptied. Look at 'em, oveflowing again! Rats everywhere but it doesn't matter 'cos we'll have the biggest transgendered opera festival in Europe. It drives me mad that in our country every year thousands of people with no talent for communicating whatsoever emerge with media studies degrees. We have the most 'educated' population ever and the stupidest television and print culture in living memory; every TV weather girl and cretinous demi-celeb has got a First from Cambridge or Georgetown, yet is the culture any more elevated than it ever was? Is it fuck. I wouldn't mind but for all his education he hadn't done any research. I think he'd just gone on the web and picked up a few soundbytes. At one stage he tried to grease up to me by telling me he was a John Lennon fan! I said, 'John Lennon, even his name makes me feel nauseous.' He practically fell off his chair! Was there ever a human being, with the possible exception of Jeffrey Archer, who was such an all-weather compendium of lies, boasts and phoniness? Working-class hero? My arse, he was about as working class as a Wilmslow dentist, unlike Paul, George, and Ringo. That's why the tosser was at art school in the early fifties, for Pete's sake! This hack said, 'What about his lyrics?' I said,

'Yes what about 'em?' *Imagine*'s lyrics sound like they came out of a stoned fortune cookie. 'Imagine no possessions'; you know at the time he wrote that him and Miss Ono kept a whole apartment in the Dakota building, just below the one they lived in, for the exclusive occupation of their fur coats. And as for The Beatles being bigger than Jesus, arse: Jesus had far better songs and didn't go about calling his Manager a 'Queer Jew'. I told him, I think the person Lennon most resembled wasn't JC but the Queen Mum, about whom it's equally impossible to imagine the BBC ever making a remotely critical programme. I think that's what Lennon actually was: a Queen Mum body double, a dry run for the burial of 'the chief leper of the leper colony' as Princess Di called her. Apologies to any lepers out there, I wouldn't want to be compared to the Windsors either.

Then to cap it all he asked me if I kept a diary! I said, 'Do I look like the kind of person who keeps a diary?' Can you imagine me sat up all night round a candle with my feather and ink? I had to read Derek Jarman's a while back 'cos I was reviewing it, that was enough to put anyone off the form for life. Why do visual artists believe they can write? I wouldn't dream of downing my typewriter, and running off to make a daubing, let alone touting it in a public place. Neither would I prance around wielding a camcorder and expect the BFI to fund me. I think Jarman's diaries were written for people who couldn't accept that *Diary of a Nobody* had no sequel, 'cos he's just like Pooter, convinced there's nothing that is so dull that it won't be improved by writing it down. I kept some of his most exciting entries on 'Post-Its' for posterity. Wait a tick.

She runs out. Returns with Jarman's Diaries *and a load of Post-Its. She reads from them.*

Here we go. 'Disturbed by a large owl. Polished the floors', 'Shopping at Sainsbury's', 'We are expecting rain. The garden could do with it', 'Bought a pullover at M&S' and 'Spent the afternoon sewing buttons on to shirts'. It's even better when he gets onto his super exciting epicurean experiments: 'Very good lunch – chops, purple cabbage and semolina', 'I cooked an excellent picnic lunch – new potatoes, ham and salad.' At one point it gets so desperate you almost expect him to write 'wrote in diary' just to break the monotony. To be honest I found all that quite funny, unintentionally, but when he turns into a queer Victor Meldrew forget it. At one point he describes people on a tube carriage as 'Thatcher's rat-faced mortgagees, not one brain cell amongst them.' Would any true artist see in a rush-hour railway carriage a seething mass of loathsomeness rather than a group of individuals with their thwarted dreams and desires? Only person who comes out of it in one piece is Neil Tennant. Apparently Jarman was going to see Jimmy Somerville and he asked Neil if he had a message for him. Tennant said, 'Tell him "Piss off, Mary, I'm Head Fairy!"' I like that! Don't go accusing me of being a homophobe for slagging off poor dead Derek – there's nothing wrong with homosexuality – I gave it a shot myself a couple of years ago, and thoroughly enjoyed it.

Puts book down.

Trouble with criticising people like Jarman or Lennon is you always get accused of being jealous of 'em. As if! They even accused me of being

jealous of Paula Yates when I had a pop at her!
I said, God, yes, how could I not have seen it all these years – forget Dorothy Parker or Ava Gardner at their prime: what I really, REALLY wanted all along was to be a suicidal, silicone-breasted, bleached-blonde, 40-year-old mother of four, who was the adulterous spawn of Hughie Green and a Bluebell Girl, with a dead boyfriend, an even deader career and a habit of being sick into her handbag at public parties. Actually I slightly regretted going over the top on Paula bashing because it wasn't her who really annoyed me, it was the sob sisters writing about her. Muriel, Justine, Jane, Deborah, Yvonne, they all had a go. The by-line was different, but the sob remained the same: 'Paula Yates Died For Our Sins'; 'Paula Yates, Innocent Victim Of A Feeding-Frenzied Media'; 'Tragic Paula, Broken Butterfly On The Wheel Of Misogyny'; 'Paula, We Hardly Knew You!'; 'What Are We Doing? What Does It Mean? Where Are We Going? Where Have We Been? What's It All About, Alfie!' Muriel Gray, who I can only hope has since been sedated, went so far as to write of Yates that she was the most powerful British female role model of our age – a role model, in a country that contains Barbara Castle, Dr Sheila Cassidy and Kate Moss. A role model whose currency was blowjobs and breast enhancement. In the words of the great Jim Royle: Arse. I can still remember the first day we met, urgh. She walked into my office at the *NME*, sat right on my desk with her legs wide apart and no knickers on, I'd never seen anything so disgusting in my life. The odd thing is that mine and her lives sorta ran parallel for a long time. We both got

married at 19 to arseholes and had children. We both lost custody of 'em and suffered endless media bullying about our suitability as mothers. In '95, we both left our husbands for more exciting young lovers. We both even went on to buy houses by the seaside. But the difference was I turned my back on London completely, Paula hung on in there, falling out of her dress at pap-infested parties and premieres. Keeping one foot in that arena meant she inevitably worried about her fading beauty, which for me was not a problem. Though I was a beautiful young women, my looks were only the icing on the cake, writing was what really mattered. The tragic thing is she was a good writer, when she could be bothered. Paula neglected her craft in favour of frocks and famous men; she expected to have an easy ride through life because she was blonde and fluffy. Being blonde and fluffy is no basis on which to build a life, Baby Doll turns to Baby Jane pretty damned quick if held a beat too long. What did Scott Fitzgerald say about his mad wife: 'Too late, she realised that work is the only dignity.' Paula, with her fantasies of being a perfect fifties homemaker, never realised this. Suicide is one of the few things that lightens my darkness. It's always there innit? That velvet roped-off area when life gets too loathsome, swinging softly in the cul de sac of my mind like a sweet chariot or safety net, a great comfort to fall back on, even better than old money.

The phone rings. She answers it.

Hello. (*It's her Editor.*) No, he's still trying to fix it. It shouldn't be long, he says he knows what the problem is. Something to do with a hard gigabyte or something. I can't fax it 'cos you see it's in the machine, I know it's awful, I'm really worried about it too. Look I better go because Dan's calling. I'll ring you as soon as he's done it. OK babe. Bye.

She puts the phone down.

I feel like having a sickie. Some weeks I'm full of ideas, others the glass is half empty. I been in this racket since I was seventeen, I'm forty-two now, I'd be lying if I said I felt as passionately about everything as I did when I started out. This hack looked at me like he'd just trod in something when I told him that. But I said to him, 'Why lie? If I pretend then I just become like most of the other columnists operating today, a phoney. Next thing you know I'll be slagging off kids for doing drugs whilst drinking myself to death, or pretending to be working class when I went to Eton or Harrow, or turning my lingering death from cancer into a cottage industry. That's why I go on about my own bad behaviour so much – to distance myself as far away from the phonies as possible. You know he then had the nerve to say, 'But isn't there a price to pay for all that pleasure Julie?' I said yes, '£5.99 for a bottle of white, £11.99 for a bottle of Absolut.' Give me the Fleet Street of old any day. At least then there were some characters around, now it's just a load of over-educated kids hoping to write themselves up a character. Blairite puritans. I got my own back at one point though: we were ordering starters and he said really pompously, 'Are you having the pumpkin soup?' and I said, 'I never eat anything with a face,' and he said, 'Are you a vegetarian?' What an arse!

She picks up the lap-top and puts it on her lap.

Can't think of anything.

Fuck it.

She puts it down. Silence. Sound of seagulls.

Sometimes when it all goes quiet like this and I'm alone I think about running away. Just packing my things and running. That's how I've always done it. I never feel so much at home as when I'm closing the door on it. That's why this house is so empty, 'cos every time I've gone I've taken nothing with me. Even now I can be walking on the seafront with the boy I love more than any other in the world and I look at him and he's so clever and beautiful, looking at me with the boldest eyes and the sweetest smile, and the sky is blue and the smell of the swimming pool is on my skin – and I still feel that something's really wrong. Then I realise what it is, I'm not alone. Whenever I see myself I'm walking away, from the slamming doors of my teenage to the moonlight flits from my marriages, I see myself forever leaving. I'm not particularly proud of this. But that's the way it is. Other people dream of leaving, I leave so I can go on dreaming. I'm terrified of getting drawn into the quicksand of the everyday, of the life less lived. And it's so easy innit, one minute you're just batting along, the next you're wondering what happened to five years of your life. When I left Tony, I walked out of our bungalow with nothing more than a bottle of amyl nitrate, a g-string, a bust of Lenin and an attitude. I remember standing on Billericay railway station with all my possessions tied up in a little hankie and I looked around me. There were all these old ladies and housewives: I just wanted to run amok and push 'em all onto the track. They were all so good, so straight and yet so depressed. And there was me, so bad and yet so full of life and so happy. No doubt they'd say, 'We'll have the last laugh.' Yeah, but I think we know who'll have had the best fucking time ever by the time we turn up our toes! I like to think that I've changed a bit now and that I won't keep running forever. Keeping on running when you've got arthritis and a Zimmer frame somehow doesn't have the desperado glamour of being a teenage runaway does it? But I'm not sure if leopards can change their spots. I got told off at both my weddings for laughing, It was the line 'forsaking all others' that did it. I suppose in my heart I think love is a lemming, death is what keeps it going. The death of love is perfectly natural; and no reflection whatsoever on the quality of it. Why is longevity the last word, who's better, the Sex Pistols lasting three years or the Stones lasting three hundred?

The phone rings.

Hi babe where are you? Oh right. Yeah, thanks. It seems to be fine. No, not yet, just trying to come up with something. Dunno. Listen how d'you fancy driving to Torquay? We could stay at the Imp. Yeah? Yeah whenever, OK babe, bye.

Puts phone down.

This hack at lunch asked me if I was as happy as I always say I am. I said I'm happier. He said, 'But after all that's happened to you: divorces, losing custody of your children, your parents dying.' I said, 'Yes I've had disappointments but I got over 'em.' I spent fifty thousand pounds fighting custody on my son but when I lost I thought it was probably for the best (amazing innit, you can suck off twenty men and get away with it but go down on one woman and they take your kids away). And I wasn't upset when my father died, he was the man I loved more than any human being ever, but I wasn't upset because I knew he had to go. Same with my Mum, she phoned me up and I went round to see her, went into the kitchen to open a tin of salmon and when I came back into the living room she was gone. I phoned 999 and the operator said give her the kiss of life and I got her friend in from next door, I knew it was time for her to go. Course if that's your attitude these days people just accuse you of being in some kind of denial. Oh yes, every attempt to put a rosy spin on this vale of tears, be it drink, drugs or watching *Eastenders* is classed as denial by those carpet bagging parasites, the counsellors. In truth it's them who are in denial, denying life is tough and painful and moping around doesn't do anyone any good. Don't forget, shrinks are called that because their aim is to shrink the magnificent sewer of the human psyche, rendering us all into neat, clean, manageable euro-portions. In my opinion the over-examined life ends up not worth living. Too many people these days mistake disappointment for depression. I have often felt disappointment because I'd spent all my money on confectionery and had nothing left to pay the taxman with, but I'd never claim that this was an illness that needed treating. It wasn't. I'm just greedy. I think depression is what the middle classes have instead of sadness. What really annoys me about therapy is the whole idea that your problems are unique to you; that they might be a reasonable reaction to racial, sexual or class-based oppression is never considered. Change has to start with you: looking in, never reaching out. Counselling is the exact opposite of socialism; no wonder it started to be so eagerly proffered by every last agent of social control just at the same time as union rights were being destroyed. It may seem liberal and humane to call alcoholism and anorexia illnesses, but if you do so, you're denying that human beings have free will, and the ability to make their own choices about the way they live their lives. It's like when I tell people that I enjoy wasting my talent, they don't believe me, they think I have some kind of illness or 'self loathing issues'. Dun half make me laugh: you can leave your children, dump your spouse and put your parents out to grass on a sex farm and still get away with it in reasonably bohemian circles, but the minute you admit to betraying your talent there is the most ridiculous amount of teeth gnashing and moralising, usually from those who never had any talent themselves in the first place. Always reminds me of poor Salieri beseeching God to give the gift to him and not that moronic and dim-minded creature Mozart. I know that I've become a reckless parody of myself but I like it. I sometimes think I'm more a standup comic than a journalist. I think I'd have become one if there'd been women like Jo Brand around when I was growing up. But in those days women were for laughing at, not with. John Updike said: 'Fame is a mask that eats the face.' That's how it's been for me, but in a good way. To begin with I used to just play Julie Burchill, then eventually I became her, now the mask won't come off, this is the real thing. But it's what I always wanted, not the money – tho'

I don't mind the money – but the fame. The fact that my heroes know my name means far more to me than any number of digits on my pay check. It takes me right back to all those teenage nights when I used to cry myself to sleep in my bedroom because Mark Bolan didn't know who I was. I always knew I had to become someone to become myself. I read a brilliant biography of Kurt Cobain recently, poor Kurt, too late he discovered fame was the last thing he really wanted. But I got what I wanted and what a whole lot of young women from my class deserve if they can find it in themselves to believe. So yes Mr Hack, why wouldn't I be happy? I'd be a bit mad if I wasn't happy. I always like what Joseph Heller said: 'Success and failure are both difficult to endure. Along with success come drugs, divorce, fornication, bullying, meditation, medication, depression, neurosis and suicide. With failure comes failure.' It's the perfect antidote to all those self-loathing pronouncements from the likes of Truman Capote and Oscar Wilde. Getting what you want is nothing less than wonderful and don't let anyone tell you otherwise.

That's why I did that interview today because I know what it's like if there's no-one to show you the way out. I went back to my old school in Bristol the other day to do a documentary. I felt like Nelson Mandela visiting Robben Island. Literally I did. Just so relieved to get out. If I'd stayed in Bristol I'd have got fucked, got pregnant, got married and after that I wouldn't have got anything but old. That's why it infuriates me when people say there's no longer a working class, and Blair declares we're all middle class now. Being working class is not just about a standard of living, it's a state of mind. You know sometimes even now I'll start saying something really opinionated, and then think, 'What the fuck am I doing? I'm a working-class girl from Somerset' and I sort of dwindle out – then towards the end I think, 'Fuck it, I'm Julie Burchill!' then I get really loud again – like a stripper doin' a high kick from behind the curtain. I still get letters from teenagers asking how I did it and I still enjoy telling them: By not going to Journalism School, not getting an education, and not training in the provinces as the NUJ still advises. As I said to this git today, I think the secret of my success is I didn't join the pop press because I wanted to be a pop star or buy drinks for pop stars or to present a TV pop programme but because I actually wanted to write. These days people seem to think words are these easily-led bimbos that you can just use to get you where you wanna go. It's not like that, words are as smart as you and me. Roger Scruton once said reading me was like reading someone who is taking her knickers off and throwing them in your face. I like that! I think that's what writing ought to be, especially if it's the reader who ends up feeling undressed. There's only one way to go if you wanna be a real success, and that's feet first into the legend.

The phone rings. She presses it onto ansaphone.

Sometimes I think about telling my editor that Julie Burchill is away for good. I have fantasies about opening a little perfume shop down on the front. Or running away to Spain. I could be the first famous Briton to leave the country because I objected that taxes weren't high enough. I think the Costa Del Sol would suit me with all the crime and drugs. I could get a villa and become a 'character' and open a bar. Call it 'Julieland' and have pictures of my past triumphs on the walls! Or I could open a counter-culture theme pub called The Zeitgeist Arms and have pictures of Punks on one wall and New Romantics on the other. I could get loads of washed-up eighties singers to do Karaoke versions of themselves. And I'd tell all my friends in England they could come and visit me, but I wouldn't mean it.

You know I have a recurring dream. In this dream I'm back in Butlin's in Bognor. The camp's deserted and I'm chasing something. I run through the deserted swimming pool with the glass roof, past the abandoned crazy golf course, the broken down merry-go-round with the horses, through the Beachcomber Lounge where the swimmers' legs move in eerie autonomy, through the glass panels on the wall around the outdoor pool where we finally catch the pirate and push him to his watery end. But everything's in the wrong place now and I can never find my way home. If I had to say when I was happiest, it was probably during the family holidays I spent at Butlin's Bognor Regis in the sixties and seventies. I tell you, the old King wouldn't have said 'Bugger Bognor' on his deathbed if they'd had a Butlin's there then, he'd have risen from it, rolled up his trousers and entered the knobbly knees contest or had a quick round of crazy golf. If Socialism is the bread of life, then crazy golf is the jam on it!

Someone once interviewed me and said I had to kill Julie Burchill in order to become her. It's a nice idea but I'm not sure if I could. I know I'm the oldest juvenile lead in the business but it's all I've ever done with my life. I'm a one-trick pony and I don't know how to do anything else. Lynn Barber said I should take some time off and spend a long time reading like when I was a child. I said it sounds like a beautiful dream Lynn but I don't think it's me. In the end of the day, I've had such a good deal. I often feel like Dame Edna when she says, 'Welcome to my gorgeous life.' I was a girl who was meant to go into a biscuit factory but I escaped. No-one else did, they've all been made into biscuits.

Car pulls up outside. Toots horn.

That'll be Dan, ready to whisk me off to Torquay down the motorway.

She looks at her coat, then goes to the door.

(*Calling off.*) I still got my column to finish. I'll be ten minutes. Fifteen tops. Go to the shop and get me a copy of *Heat* for the journey please. And some nice chocolates.

She comes back in.

Much as I like perfume, 'The Fragrant Julie Burchill' doesn't quite ring true, does it? Besides, how many customers would I have left after I'd told 'em what I really thought of their outfits every day?! And I'd only end up losing my nose from skin cancer if I moved to the Costa Del Sol.

She picks up the lap-top.

What shall I write about? Any ideas?

She suddenly has an idea. Starts typing.

Now Dan's mended the 'I' key it seems a shame not to use it.

She types some more.

Who knows, this time I might even tell you the truth.

She continues to hammer out the column as the lights fade to black.

Ends.

A Nick Hern Book

Julie Burchill is Away . . . first published in Great Britain in 2002 as a paperback original by Nick Hern Books Ltd, 14 Larden Road, London W3 7ST, in association with Fat Bloke Productions

Typeset by Country Setting, Kingsdown, Kent, CT14 8ES
Printed and bound in Great Britain by Bookmarque, Croydon, Surrey

ISBN 1 85459 675 6

A CIP catalogue is available from the British Library